Octopuses

Octopuses

Jenny Markert

THE CHILD'S WORLD®, INC.

Published in the United States of America by The Child's World®, Inc.
PO Box 326
Chanhassen, MN 55317-0326
800-599-READ
www.childsworld.com

Product Manager Mary Berendes
Editor Katherine Stevenson
Designer Mary Berendes
Contributor Bob Temple

Photo Credits
ANIMALS ANIMALS © Fleetham, D. OSF: 9, 20
ANIMALS ANIMALS © Zig Leszczynski: 13
© Anthony Mercheca, The National Audubon Society Collection/Photo Researchers: 10 (small photo)
© 2001 Bob Cranston/Mo Yung/www.norbertwu.com: 23 (main photo)
© 2001 Brandon D. Cole: 2, 15, 16
© C. Ray, The National Audubon Society Collection/Photo Researchers: 19
© Eiichi Kurasawa/www.norbertwu.com: 29
© 2001 Jeff Rotman/Stone: cover
© Marilyn & Maris Kazmers/SharkSong: 6, 24, 30
© 2001 Norbert Wu/www.norbertwu.com: 23 (small photo), 26
© 2001 Stuart Westmorland/Stone: 10 (main photo)

Library of Congress Cataloging-in-Publication Data
Markert, Jenny.
Octopuses / by Jenny Markert.
p. cm.
Includes index.
ISBN 1-56766-890-9 (library bound : alk. paper)
1. Octopus—Juvenile literature. [1. Octopus.] I. Title.
QL430.3.O2 M37 2001
594'.56—dc21
00-010802

On the cover...

Front cover: This giant Pacific octopus is swimming at night.
Page 2: This giant Pacific octopus is hard to see as it rests among other sea plants and animals.

Table of Contents

Far beneath the ocean's surface, a clam sits on the ocean bottom. Fish swim back and forth, paying no attention. But behind a rock, a strange-looking creature with eight "arms" is watching the clam closely. Quietly it slides out from behind the rock. Then its eight arms quickly grab the clam and pry it open—and the clam becomes dinner. What is this unusual eight-armed animal? It's an octopus!

What Do Octopuses Look Like?

An octopus's body is very different from yours. It doesn't have bones or a skeleton. Instead, it is soft and baglike. The octopus's head is tiny and has eyes on top. An octopus can see backwards without even turning its head!

The octopus's most striking feature is its eight armlike **tentacles.** The word "octopus" comes from a Greek word that means "eight-footed one." Strangely, an octopus's tentacles are attached to its head, not its body. These long, muscular tentacles can coil and twist in any direction. Under each tentacle are rows of suction cups that can cling to rocky walls and slippery food. Most octopuses have more than 200 suction cups on each tentacle.

This day octopus has its tentacles spread wide as it swims near Hawaii. ⇒

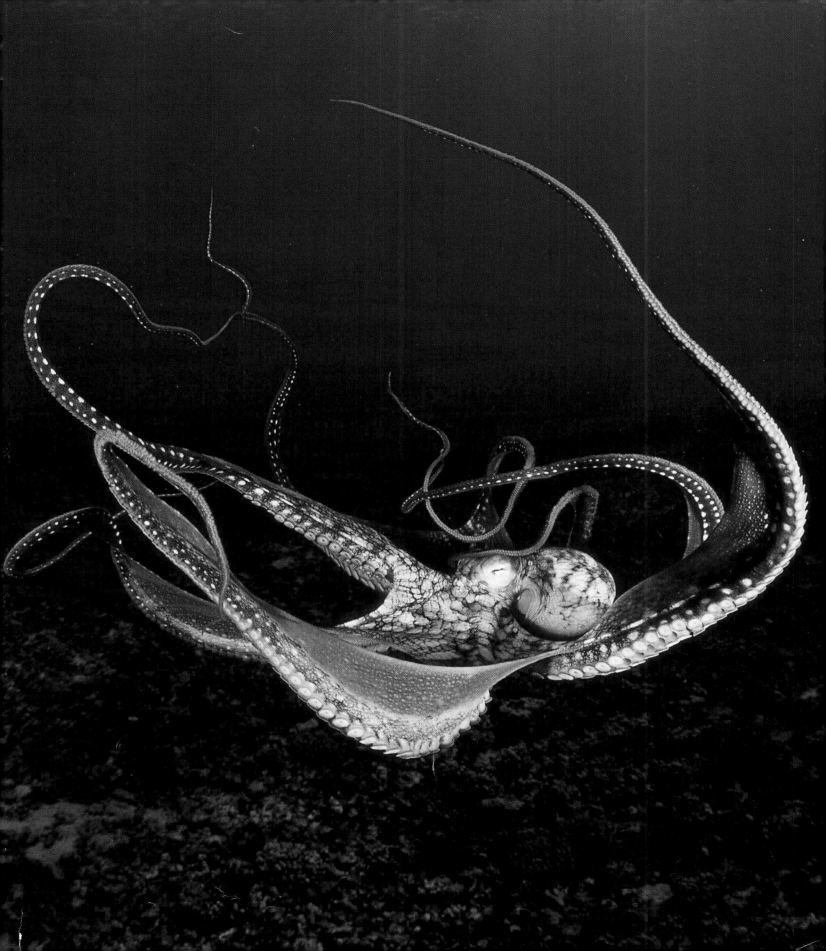

Are There Different Kinds of Octopuses?

There are about 200 different kinds, or **species,** of octopuses. They live throughout the world's oceans, from warm coral reefs to the frozen seas of Antarctica. Most octopuses live in shallow water. But one type of octopus lives two miles beneath the ocean surface!

Octopuses vary greatly in size. The smallest type is the *Californian octopus.* It only grows to be about 1 inch long. *Common octopuses* are about the size of a skateboard. The *giant Pacific octopus* is the largest type. It can grow over 20 feet long from the tip of one tentacle to the tip of the other. That's as long as a school bus!

⇐ *Main photo:* This giant Pacific octopus is swimming in the open ocean.
Small photo: This tiny Californian octopus is resting on a sea plant.

Are Octopuses Dangerous?

Octopuses might look scary, but in real life they are mainly shy, harmless animals. They would much rather sneak away than attack a person. Like other animals, however, octopuses can be dangerous when they are bothered or frightened.

One type, called the *blue-ringed octopus*, is very dangerous. Normally this small octopus is a brownish color with dull blue rings. When it becomes angry or excited, it turns yellow with bright blue spots. When it bites, this octopus shoots poisonous **venom** into its attacker. Just a small amount of venom from a blue-ringed octopus can kill a person in less than two hours!

This blue-ringed octopus is resting in a coral reef. ⇒
The dull blue color of its spots shows that it is calm.

Are Octopuses Smart?

Octopuses are very smart animals. Sometimes an octopus runs into a problem, such as getting food from a hard-to-reach area. It will try many different ways of solving the problem. Once the octopus succeeds, it remembers the answer for the next time it faces the same problem.

This mimic octopus has learned a trick to attract fish. It hides its ⇒ whole body except for two tentacles and its eyes. Then it changes its color to look like a sea snake. When a hungry fish swims by to eat the "snake," the octopus leaps out and catches it!

Regardless of their size, octopuses are very shy and secretive. They prefer to live alone. They make their homes, called **dens,** in rocky caves, coral reefs, and shipwrecks. Small octopuses live in empty seashells. Some even live in human garbage such as pop bottles or tin cans. Octopuses leave their dens only to avoid a nosy enemy or to find food.

⇐ Here you can see a giant Pacific octopus's tentacle as it feels around the entrance to its den. The empty scallop shells are from past meals.

17

What Do Octopuses Eat?

Octopuses like to eat many different kinds of sea creatures. Sometimes an octopus collects a pile of oysters or clams. Then it uses its suction cups to pull the shells apart and get to the food inside. Octopuses also eat crabs and lobsters.

Octopuses have a beak that looks a bit like a parrot's. The octopus uses its sharp beak to break through the animal's shell. Then it kills the animal with a dose of poison the octopus makes in its mouth. The poison also softens the animal's flesh so the octopus can suck up its meal.

This giant Pacific octopus has caught a crab to eat. The octopus is ⇒ using its suction cups and tentacles to bring the crab up to its beak.

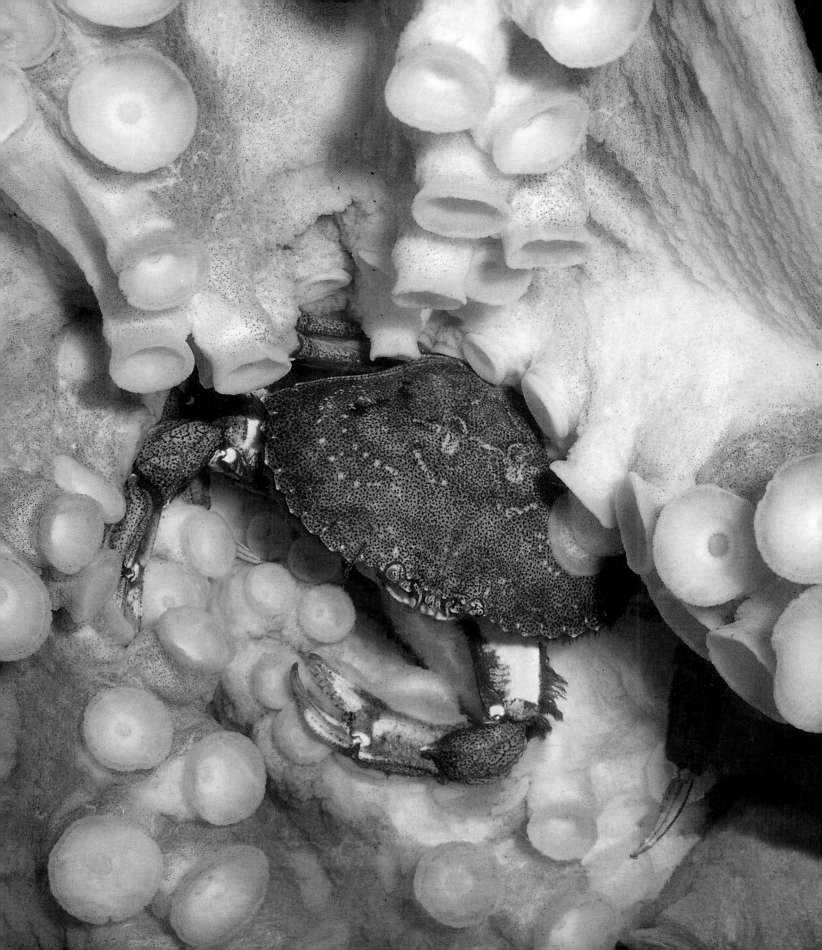

How Do Octopuses Swim?

Octopuses also have ways of catching faster prey. From its den or a hiding place, an octopus can bolt out and grab a passing fish. Octopuses are fast swimmers and can dart back and forth in any direction. Beneath an octopus's head is a pouch called a **mantle.** When the octopus wants to swim quickly, its mantle swells up like a water balloon. Then strong muscles push the water out through a special tube called a **siphon.** The rushing water pushes the octopus forward or backward like a rocket.

⇐ This day octopus is swimming off the coast of Hawaii.

What Are Baby Octopuses Like?

Besides using their dens for hiding, female octopuses use them for raising their young. After mating, a female lays thousands of eggs—sometimes 200,000 or more! She strings the eggs along the walls of her den. Each egg is about the size and shape of a grain of rice. After she lays all of the eggs, the female octopus stays nearby, protecting and cleaning them.

After about one month, the tiny babies hatch. But they must learn to live on their own—their mother dies soon after her eggs hatch. From the moment they are born, baby octopuses are faced with danger. They are as tiny as fleas and cannot swim. They drift in the ocean, hoping to avoid hungry sea creatures. Only a few baby octopuses are lucky enough to survive until their first birthday.

Main photo: This female giant Pacific octopus is guarding her eggs. ⇒
Small Photo: These California two-spot octopus eggs are starting to hatch.

How Do Octopuses Stay Safe?

Even as adults, octopuses still face many dangers. Large fish, seals, and moray eels like to eat octopuses. Luckily, octopuses are great escape artists. Special coloring called **camouflage** helps them blend in with their surroundings and hide from their enemies. Octopuses are commonly white with red or gray dots. Next to coral or rocky sea bottoms, they are very hard to see.

⇐ This common octopus is very hard to see as it sits on the ocean floor near Florida.

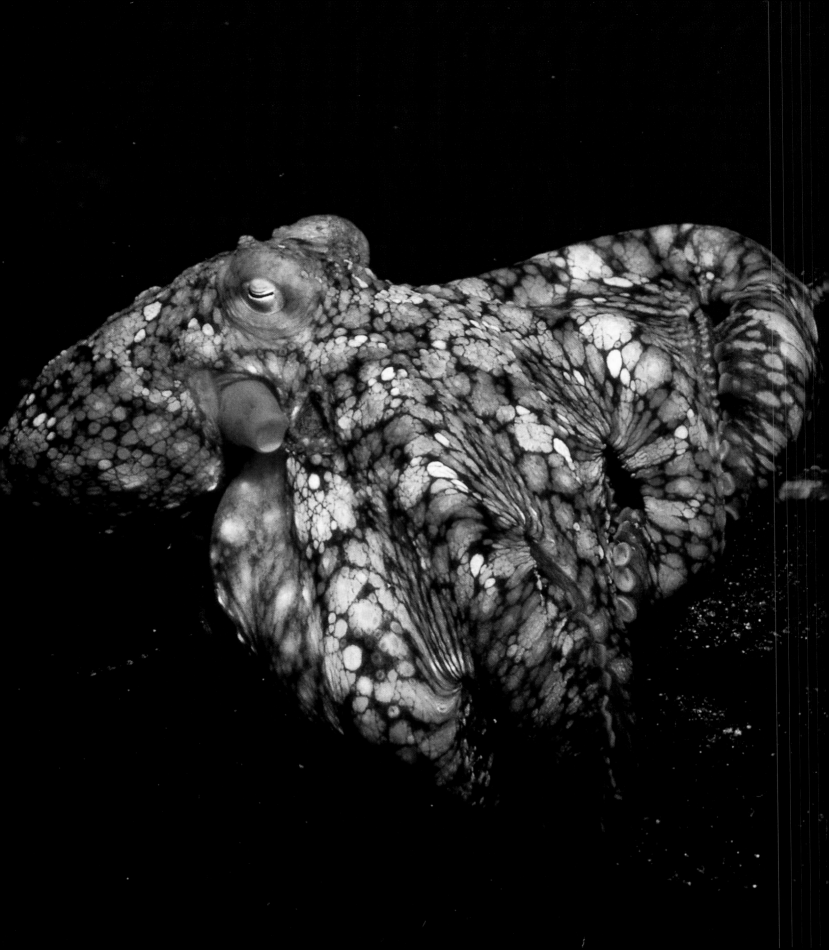

If an enemy does see an octopus, the octopus can actually change colors! A whole wave of different colors can flow across its skin. The octopus can turn red, green, or even black. The octopus's skin can also change patterns, showing stripes, solid colors, or dots.

Scientists think that octopuses also change colors to show their moods. Frightened octopuses turn pale, light colors. Angry octopuses are solid purple or black. When they eat, octopuses are often colored with spots and blotches.

⇐ You can see many different colors and shapes in
the skin of this two-spotted octopus. It is changing
colors to match some nearby seaweed.

Even if the octopus's show of colors doesn't confuse its enemy, the octopus has another trick. Instead of staying around to fight, it makes a clever escape. When the enemy attacks, the octopus squirts a dark, inky liquid into the water. The cloud of ink looks and smells like the octopus. When the enemy attacks, it finds only an inky blob. Meanwhile, the octopus darts away to safety.

This small octopus off the coast of Japan is releasing ⇒
ink to get away from the photographer.

Octopuses might live in hidden caves and sunken ships, but they aren't the monsters we imagine them to be. These shy, harmless animals have many clever ways of avoiding danger and catching food. In fact, they are one of the most fascinating of all Earth's undersea creatures!

⇐ Here a giant Pacific octopus swims in
a kelp forest near British Colombia.

Glossary

camouflage (KAM-oo-flahj)
Camouflage is special coloring or markings that help an animal look like its surroundings. Camouflage coloring helps octopuses hide against the sea bottom.

dens (DENZ)
A den is a hollow or hidden spot where an animal makes its home. Octopuses make their dens in caves, rocks, or other protected places.

mantle (MAN-tull)
The mantle of an octopus is a balloonlike sac or bag of flesh that the octopus fills with water. An octopus's mantle is beneath its head.

siphon (SY-fun)
Some animals have a breathing tube called a siphon. Octopuses use their siphon like a jet engine, forcing water through it to push themselves through the water.

species (SPEE-sheez)
A species is a different kind of an animal. There are about 200 different octopus species.

tentacles (TEN-teh-kullz)
Tentacles are soft, bendable body parts that some animals have instead of arms. Octopuses have eight tentacles.

venom (VEN-um)
Venom is a poison that some animals make in their bodies. Octopuses make venom in their mouths.

Web Sites

http://www.aqua.org/animals/species/procto.html

http://www.marinelab.sarasota.fl.us/OCTOPI.HTM

http://www.underwater.com.au/octopus.html

Index